The Pet Fun Run

By Sally Cowan

It is the fun run for pets!

Pip can hop.

Rib can jog.

And Mits and Bib
can run and run.

Pets!

Get set! **Go!**

Pip hops and hops.

But Rib can go!

Rib jogs and jogs.

Bib runs up to Rib the rat.

Bib bit Rib!

Rib got a bad cut!

Mits jogs up to Bib.

Bib can see Mits.

Mits is a **big** dog.

Bib ran and hid!

Mits runs in to the mud.

Mits had fun in the mud!

Pip hops and hops.

Pip had fun!

CHECKING FOR MEANING

1. Who can jog in the fun run? *(Literal)*

2. What does Mits have fun in? *(Literal)*

3. Why did Bib run away from Mits? *(Inferential)*

EXTENDING VOCABULARY

hop	Look at the word *hop*. How many sounds are in the word? How does a rabbit hop? What other animals do you know that hop?
bad	What does *bad* mean? Which word is the opposite of *bad*? If you change the *a* to *e*, what new word would you make?
big	Re-read the sentence, *Mits is a **big** dog*. What is another word that means the same as *big* and could be used in this sentence?

MOVING BEYOND THE TEXT

1. How are fun runs for people the same or different to this pet fun run?

2. Why do people like being in races?

3. Have you ever been in a fun run? Did you enjoy it? Why?

4. What other outdoor activities can you do for fun?

SPEED SOUNDS

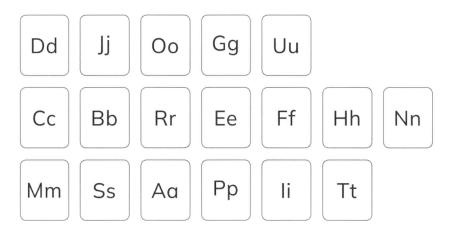

Dd	Jj	Oo	Gg	Uu		
Cc	Bb	Rr	Ee	Ff	Hh	Nn
Mm	Ss	Aa	Pp	Ii	Tt	

PRACTICE WORDS

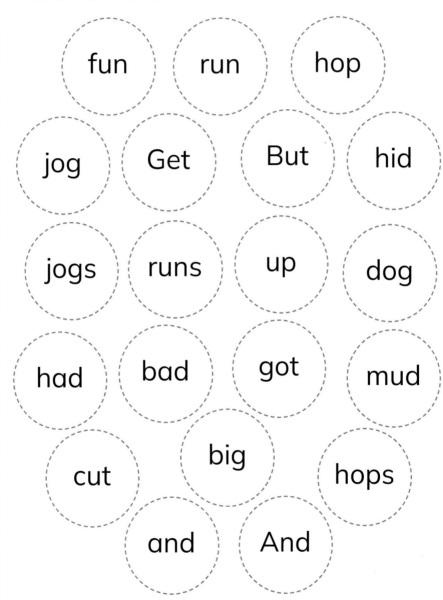

fun

run

hop

jog

Get

But

hid

jogs

runs

up

dog

had

bad

got

mud

cut

big

hops

and

And